Wing
QUAINTRELLE'S
MERAKI

A K S H A Y A C 4 R O X

© Akshayac4rox 2022

All rights reserved

All rights reserved by author. No part of this publication may be reproduced, stored in a retrieval system or transmitted in any form or by any means, electronic, mechanical, photocopying, recording or otherwise, without the prior permission of the author.

Although every precaution has been taken to verify the accuracy of the information contained herein, the author and publisher assume no responsibility for any errors or omissions. No liability is assumed for damages that may result from the use of information contained within.

First Published in July 2022

ISBN: 978-93-5628-294-0

BLUEROSE PUBLISHERS
www.BlueRoseONE.com
info@bluerosepublishers.com
+91 8882 898 898

Cover Design:

for the daydreamers,
for the night thinkers,
those who crave voyage,
those who seek solace,
to the skinny dippers,
to the shiftless sloth bears
who flips through marketing magazines
who reads fiction with a brew of caffeine
for the hearts who party all night,
for the souls who gazes at the stars
to the dreamers, believers, and fighters
to someone who's a little bit of everything
~from one of the chunks of your tribe

ACKNOWLEDGMENT

Mom

I couldn't be more grateful to you for making this book come true. Just know something, nothing would have been here in this way if not for you. Not me. Not my book. Not my life. You believed in me even when I'm bereft of hope and stood by me through everything. You are my sand, my root, my sunlight and now I am blooming. You're are my mother, my best friend, my soulmate. With you by my side, I need no one else. I love you!

Northern Star

How can someone make me feel understood, comforted, and loved being miles afar? You made feel all of it. I never met you, but I can feel your presence in my heart. You watered my words, bestowing me the courage to endure the world full of flawed people with black coats. The sheer mention of your name, mere minute of your

In addition to that, I explored myself, and developed a newfound passion to play with words, flirt with metaphors, and tease with similes. It transported me to the portal, to an alternate reality, not the one I can barely live in but the one where I can create and control.

Bluerose team

Having a dream is one thing but watching it shape in front of your eyes is something incredible.

The Bluerose publishers, Asha (new agent), Alisha (old agent), Shruti (Manager), Deepika (Assistant manager), Namrata (Typographic)

A special thanks to all the amazing people who enabled me to turn this collection of poetry into an incredibly framed book.

AUTHOR'S NOTE

One day she realized it's not just leisure; penning down her tales, eliciting the people in the spotless canvas of her uncanny mind. It enclosed the essence of herself, unleashed the wings of her soul, wielded her raw emotions. It's not her escape from the real world it's an entrance to her realm, where she can be fierce, fearless, and flawed. It was her way of expressing, assuring, and promising herself; she's enough. Everyone said she can't fit in their world. They didn't know she had no desire to fit in. She didn't seek a place in their world instead she created her realm. Her voice echoed in the pages of the book. It's not just the words. It's her world.

~this is she

elements

vagary 1

hygge 20

virago 42

saudade 71

hiraeth 104

metanoia 137

vagary

(n.) an unpredictable instance, a wandering journey; a whimsical, wild, unusual idea, desire, or action.

I'm a lost star
half a way between
torn apart in conflict
to go back
from where I've begun
or to go-ahead
to where I'd ended up

Is she stubborn,
grumpy,
snappy,
clingy,
aggressive,
envious?
Oh, don't be so certain
It's her existence that's uncertain.

Her life is the sum of anxiety
That makes her brain quite hazy
She wants to make friends
But she doesn't go with the trends
Her jealousy is unimaginable
But the comparison with classmates is manageable
She wants to go on a Manali trek
But who knew she's a nervous wreck?
God forbid all the books and movies
That stimulated all her stupid fantasies

Her heart is hard to carry after the dark

She's judged for what she did
Yet bullied for what she didn't
She doesn't have time for her passion and goals
'Cause she's caught up in the web of who likes her and who all don't
Once in a Blue Moon, to her parents, she wants to talk
'Back in my time...' is all she got
She's so insecure
Someone, please find the goddamn cure
Her life is the never-ending conflict of 'speak up' and 'shut up'
No wonder she finds their rules hard to pick up
Sometimes she feels lost
Sometimes she exists like a ghost
Don't be so mean
She is damn seventeen

People say this is the golden year
But only she knew she wants to disappear
She's ripped apart from the safety of the childhood
She's stuffed into the timberland of adulthood

This is the generation of
eloping kids,
abandoning parents,
confused minds,
broken people,
fake friendships,
void promises,
scarred souls,
but what do we do?

Parents pressure us for ranks
Friends pressure us for pranks
Cousins torture us with our hoards
Teachers torture us with our boards

Our heads spin like a Ferris wheel
Oh, wait it's no big a deal
We are expected to be honest
But handled not just
We have no choice
We shouldn't raise our voice

But we carry within ourselves the light of hidden blossoms
We could have been the right people
If we are born in a right generation

Maybe we are the right people
Born at the wrong generation

One December night, the moon was shining bright
I was sitting in my room, seeking some dim light
It's supposed to be sedated
Until my time in your presence disputed
Your voice like nails on the chalkboard echoed in my ears
Your words like knives cut the self-esteem I constructed through years
I tried to block you 'cause I can never impress you
Maybe one day I'll find my words again

You were hell-bent on pointing to my flaws again and again
Rubbing salt on my fresh wounds over and over again
When I tried to speak up you pushed my voice down my throat
Shooting your hurtful words, that I couldn't find mine anymore
Maybe one day I'll find my words again

I was just a thirteen-year-old girl
Squirming under your words,

Your brutal words still make me cold
Maybe one day I'll find my words again

I'm just seventeen, but I am sure of one thing
Sometime in the distant future
You will be the same girl with a loud mouth and void opinions
At the food counter at the office party, standing alone
All washed up and still ranting about how
You're better than the girl in the pink dress
But all you are is just a mean, pathetic parasite sucking out other's self-esteem

But someday I'll be having a life I dreamt of
In a coffee shop hanging out with my real friends
Chatting about the weather, ranting about the cricket match, arguing about the fanfiction
Where my inner voice overpowered your screeches,
Your little stares don't ruin my days
Your mean comment doesn't haunt my good-night sleep

Disney land to timberland
Tons and tons of cruel demand
All of 'em a haze to understand
Dangerously difficult to withstand
Struggling for a brand, disobeying the command
Future being unplanned, anxiety being on remand

I walked through the revolving door
Iced feet grazing the floor
Adrenaline surging from the core
Like the seals have come ashore
Unaware of what the future has in store
Here I'm dying to explore

Future is a clumsy route
Still trying to figure this out
I ain't sure what I want, don't ask me!
Yet here I keep walking down this road,
Unknown; where it'll take me?
I feel scared to go alone
Though I have nothing to atone

This and that carved on display
Strikingly nigher yet distinctly away
Either of them tempting with their allure
With my poor soul yearning to assure

Trying to figure out what's true and what isn't
Closure felt more than distant
Trying to hide my scarlet fears
Wiping away my secret tears
I strive to write what I dream
'Cause my voice is a low-key scream
I've thrived to dream what I write
'Cause my mind is not always quite

I tried to take the road that's less travelled by
That lead me to a locked castle thereby—
Amplifying the dream and presumptions of a bourgeoisie—
For that, all of my attempts have been the false key

I'm assured I would fit in

I'm just a small-town girl
Living in this crazy world

I know;
Maybe I'll be wrong
But life will go on
I should be strong
I can't stop but move on
At least a hundred miles afar
Towards whatever opportunity ajar

'Cause I'm just a small-town girl
Living in this crazy world
Leasing the wings of words
Dreaming to fly like the birds
I'm just a small-town girl
Living in this crazy world

People say teenage is the golden year
But it's a short infinity of utter despair
Every trivial thing hit on your chest like a rock
Every star in the sky explode in your veins with a shock
Every joy and sorrow drench you like rain
Every hormone in your body flushed towards your brain
Stimulating a grand explosion like never before
Everything will be heightened as thousand more

One low grade tightens your chest
One smile from your crush twists and turns your gut
One day without your best friend is an eternity of solitude
One simple family feud puts you in a solemn mood
Nothing remarkable ever happen to you
But still, go, strike another match, start anew

Like as not it's better so
You may never know...

Am I a mere girl born into this world?
Else a darling possession as a lustrous jewel?
Am I a good daughter and sister to my family?
Else the one to make my friends laugh gaily?
Am I an artist who paints the world?
Else a musician to whose rhythm you twirl?
Am I a writer who makes your hearts flutter?
Else a spectator in the crowd that mutter?
For that life is too short to choose
To be what or to be whose?

Waking up to a pool of blood
A million things running in my head
With cramps and pangs
Twitches and twinges
Discomfort and aches in the places I never felt
Everything in my mind was amplified
And expired at all once
I'm overwhelmed yet bereft
Is it me or my mind playing tricks?
A sharp pain surged up through my veins
Draining the blood from them for a change
Heart scampered; mind whimpered
Eyes full of tears, mind full of fears
Of the known yet wanting it to be unknown
Am I too young or too old?
Soon I'll be decked up with gold
Barely remembering the contacts of a med

This or that...
I couldn't decide
I don't know which one to choose
They have both what I want and need
Tempting my greed
If I choose one
Then I'll lose the other
That sting in my brain
Pulling it from either side like a tether
Nothing in this world comes for free
But I don't want to have them at each other's cost
One has the comfort of a homeland
The other, the adventure of a timberland
Which one should I choose?
Sweetest realities — or

The buttons of my shirt tangled in my straight hair
My mind was a hedge maze about how I dare
To leave the place where I grew
For the adventures that made my heart groove
Just like a foolish maiden
I realized all of a sudden
You won't be there
When I get sick
When I wanna speak
You won't be there for me to seek
The very thought made me go weak
In the hostel room, I had no courage to tell you I was scared
That was the first time we were there
From here for the first time,
You go home without me
The scenery from the window was mesmerizing
But not enough to distract me from our home's balcony railing

There I lay in my flannel

Short fuse, got to dismantle
Plume-less biped still
Like a reserved golden quill
Emotions deeper than the ocean
Thoughts like the distorted sand
Some are creepy and weird
Some held memories of the dear
Each of 'em, all of 'em
Striking all at once—like
Waves hitting the shore
Heart yearning for more
Brain was scared
Heart was dared
Every bone in me implored me to explore
Every nerve of mine hid all the anxiety indoor
Loneliness crept into my veins
All my childhood fear crawled into my sense
I'm confused, what to say?
I'm confused, who should I listen to?
'Cause in the screaming silence

Teenage is a selcouth
Your body feels alive
Your mind never falls asleep
You will be dancing in the clouds
Singing melodies with the stars
Dopamine and oxytocin flushed into your brain
Causing blissful feelings of love to rain
You will feel like the five-year-old with colourful candies
The world around you will be unicorns and rainbows

But one day like all the temporary things
The candy will crack or the sweetness is a forgotten memory
The world around you is nothing but a black hole
Your misery bound you with her chains
And pull you into the apparent darkness
The heart that was once the home of light
Will be nothing but a broken fraction of darkness

Your head hurts, appetite fades

The brightest parts blinds you with merry
And the darkest ones with misery
Being young is blissful, but is also painful
Equal parts of pleasure and pain
Equally magical and miserable
Even the trivial things would feel overwhelming
Sadly, there is no way out of this
There is only a way through this

But one day like all the temporary things
The pain and sufferings will fleet away
One day it doesn't hurt anymore
The sorrow will slip away
The rock on your chest lifts
The knots in your stomach liberates
The pain in your heart eases
Until its nothing but a distant memory
A nightmare you can't recollect
But you have got to wait

It breaks your soul

hygge

(n.) the ritual of enjoying life's simple pleasure.
friends. family. graciousness.

I've always marvelled
Occasionally endeavoured
To comprehend how does she find
The energy to be everything;
A caregiver,
Driver,
Secretary,
Teacher,
Listener,
Therapist,
Well-wisher,
A best friend,
A lover without heartbreak
How can a soul
love another pouring their entire body, heart, mind, and soul,

The sunrises, the sunsets
The moon grows, the moon recedes
Earth spins, seasons change
The cosmos coincides, and the universe evolves
You remain there radiant, gleaming bright,
Unwavering
And bestowing the direction, an ally to find the way home
In the changing world, you are my constant
Without you I'm directionless
~you're my northern star

I can live without romantic love
But the love my girls have for me.
Is just as different
They are the madness I crave
They are the sanity I need
To survive
The way we understand each other
Hold irreplaceable space for each other
Is of a kind
~Rare

When the sky kisses the ocean
The hues of blues fused
As they hold onto each other
Like star crossed soulmates
Who aligned the stars,
For that they are not the
Montague's and Capulet's
—a royal mess
They are the species of rise and fall
Casting spells that stretch them
To infinity and beyond
~eternity is in blue

She opened her heart bare
She let him see her despair
He handled it with care
In the hope to repair
Her heart raced
At every trace that ceased
He found love
In the space that was hollow
He made himself a home
In her flesh and bone
~she is the earth and he is the tree

The soil of the wild
A sparkle of daylight smiled
A word in my head
The stars in their places
The pine trees tearing the sky
A fitting place to live and die

Deadly sins
Musical notes
Hindu's portal to salvation
Buddha's steps at his inception
Christian testament of god's ease
Islam's symbol of infinity and space
Sisters in the Pleiades star cluster
Disney princess' little misters
Stages to attain the revival
Stellar objects that are visible
Steps around the fire to convene
Sum of colours in a rainbow
Number of days in a week
Continents and seas on the earth
Wonders in the ancient world
Born date of an eccentric girl

There is poetry in every blossom
A ballad in every tree
A couplet in every bush
There is a tale behind every strike of a storm

There is a lyric in every brook
A cadence in every drop of rain
A rhythm in every beat of a heart
There is an innocence in every drop of snow

The wild wings of wilful birds
Claws of paraplegic critter
Fangs of blemmyae varmint
The stagnant solace of solitary species

There is a wonder, a certain fascination
In every life that's created — sometimes
They are adorned with the jewel of words,
And left unsaid else unfeted in the other

Beauty is serene, silent, and fragile

She melds the sun and rain
She touches blue and green
She's the reflection in the droplets
She's the rays of light changing directions
She's a colourful tornado greeting the volcano
In the universe of men and miracle she's a rainbow

Give me another set of eyes to see
Ears to listen
Lips to speak
Mind to seek
Heart to feel
Words to heal
O! Mighty my lord o!
Let the creativity within me
Flow from and towards me
'Cause the artist in me never gets sick
Of being used to her crucial basic;
Seeing the beauty in every place
Tasting the poetry in every phase
Of laugh and life and love
I always wonder how
My heart says
A picture is worth a thousand words

Hues of red
Hues of blue
Changing colours
To impress each other
~sun and sky and seasons

Every month passed
Saving the best for the last
Waking up to see the blanket of snow
Dressing up with glittery blazers and bow
Playing truth or dare
Pretending the world is fair
Dancing under the Christmas lights
Waiting for the one-horse open sleighs
Celebrating the holy spirit that's striven
The entirety of our mistakes forgiven
Everything is glassy and blue
It's freezing under the blankets too
May all your wishes come true
But wish with the purest of heart for one or two
Beneath the mistletoe
Gazing at the fire glow
Moving the furniture to dance
Baby, like that, was our last chance

Decked up with gold in the dawn
Gleaming like the silver in the dusk
~sunlight

Eclectic hues of blue
Gold-silver commotion
Chaotic clouds
Waves in the sky
~a perfect morning

You're the only magic I believe in
~to my mom

The sun burns the sky
Inflicting them with scars
The moonlight arrives
Heals them, and turns them into stars

Even the sun is scared of the dark clouds
For that, when they appear in crowd
She shed light on the world
Via the moon

The sky is the enigmatic graveyard of stars
Where cryptic deaths remained unsolved

You paint me red and gold
You make me fall for you
Every time you arrive
~Leaves to autumn

Life is the smallest song
No skip, no replay
So, when you are at it
Turn up the volume
Let the rhyme sweep you off your feet
Sing at the top of your lungs
Dance like no one watching
In the concert of life
Reclaim your spotlight

Time and distance are two strange things
Strikingly nigher yet distinctly away
Along the course of it
We either blessed to grow together,
Or cursed outgrow each other
There's no in-between

virago

(n.) a strong, brave, or warlike woman; a woman who demonstrates exemplary and heroic qualities.

Her opinions are the veil on her beauty
Her scars adorn her like a gold-plated gown
Her shed tears are the jewel on her crown
World beneath her heels, she's a luminous divinity

Flawless skin like a cloudless clime
Eyes sparkles as the starry sundown
Ebony locks darker than the night
Countenance brighter than the light
An hourglass body
Fragile and delicate
She never talks back,
Will forgive you with a smile,
Will cross even a hundred miles,
Just for the gaze of your orifices
Puts herself humbly to thy ordinance
Has a body like gold, a heart-shaped tattoo
Born from an apocalypse she's a wax statue
~only a wax statue can be flawless

Your touch made me numb
Etched slashes on my body
A scarlet letter—
Inscribed my identity
~A for abused

Assault, abuse, harassment
Thousand different names for an embarrassment
She is programmed
To be careful twenty-four seven
Like it's not her life but a battle field
A field of monsters and mines
Striving to consume her
Father, brother, cousin, teacher
Friend, colleague, or an outsider
Varied connection, one brutal notion
Is it wrong that she trusted you enough to sit closer?
Didn't she resist you enough for you to get a closure?
Yet,
Her clothes and character were blamed

She's beautiful
Even on her briskest days
She watches the sunset
Gazes at the autumn leaves
Even in the days of gimmicks
Her mind tastes the poetry
Brain believed in fairy tales
Even in her darkest days
She carried the light within her soul

If you're born with the beauty of a rose
You'll be bestowed with the shield of thorns

She's the fire; you can't resist, you can't control
She's the crimson coated crack on dawn
She paints the dusk's break—cherry
Horns on the head, eyes burning red
She breathes the magic of the stars
She bathes in the stream of mountains

She's the restless voyager—an untamed spirit
She's the intuitive forager, leaves the dead buried
Hands-on the bowstring, thighs chase the wild
She brims with passion, eye forward in stride
She runs through fire and blaze to fill her soul

She's the sudden surge in the light
She's the sunniest star at night
She's the quick kiss in the dark
She's the spirit with an ignited spark
She's the confessor of sins
She's the Queen of hearts

No scheme is grand for her to acquire

She knows how to rise again
And when she's burnout
She dives deep into the earth
To be reborn

She's a dreamer, a believer, a fighter
She's the one-way street, a stereo turned up
She's a force to reckon, a force to bow
She's the woman you'd walk straight into flame for
She's the woman who burns to live
If you can't stand her then kneel

The rush of hormones painting the walls red
Fragile crystal rolling out of their satchel
Lounging there in silence for a seal
Once it's sealed a new life commences
When ceased the walls are broken down,
The fragile crystals are flushed
Through the gateway of life with cells and tissue
Washing away the tract, dyeing the skirt red
Pains and cramps in the stomach and back
Every atom of my body chewing with discomfort
The lava flowing between my legs burning the skin
Is a sacred stream, the first bathe of the human's life?
It's not the contamination, not the sin
Thermal bags tucked into my t-shirt
I'm screaming in silence
Bleeding without violence
Stop weaponizing my mood swings
Stop criticizing my cravings
For that, you don't feel a thing I felt
Tender body, trouble sleeping
Volatile mind, constantly alerting

Her creases made her beautiful
Her cracks made her whole
Her pain made her powerful
Her sufferings made her stronger
She is everything
Because of these everything

Women shine bright with
Every tear they shed,
Every battle they fought,
Every obstacle they overcame,
Every hurdle they underwent,
Every pain they endured,
Every fear they conquered,
Every demon they embraced,
Every angel they forged,
Because, darling, they are the ode
Inscribed from the ink of gold

She is the fire
She can warm you or burn you
She is the water
She can soothe you or drown you
She is the air
She can be a gentle breeze or a drastic hurricane
She is the land
She can shelter life or consign one to the grave
She can be sensitive, she can be destructive
She can protect you; she can hurt you
She can love you; she can hate you
She can do anything, she can do everything
'Cause
She's sculpted to be her hero
When the world breaks her into pieces

Voice your thoughts
Your opinions matter
Conquer your fears
You have to be brave
Fight your battle
You deserve freedom
Stand firm on your ground
You have to be stubborn
Laugh out loud
You want to be happy
Trip on your feet
You can be goofy
Soothe your soul
You deserve to be loved

She is everything real in the unreal world

They struck a match trying to scare her
Unknown to them; she's the wildfire

She's the chaos in the tranquil form

Her scars are the stars
Her blemish are the clouds
The sun is the glow on her face
The moon is the sparkle in her eyes
~she's the universe

She's the rare breed of woman
She could feel the sun in the moonlight

She's a dreamer
An over thinker
She is a mystery
A secret keeper
She's a believer
A warrior at heart

It takes at least a hundred years to achieve feminism

If a woman sees other women as an opponent

And a man as an alliance against them

Imagine what we could have achieved if we were able to walk after the dark without any fear

~every woman who's restricted to their homes

Never pretend to be less intelligent
For a man, so that
He could feel competent around you
Never pretend to be weak
For a man, so that
He could feel strong around you
Never pretend to be anything lesser than what you are
For a man, so that
He could feel anything more than he is
'Cause the real one will be proud, not embarrassed
The real one will be inspired not threatened
And the real one doesn't fake it or pretend
The real one will be real

No man is worth the energy you spend on hating yourself

Do you cry about the hair fall
while paying a hundred or thousand
to remove it from your body?
Do you talk about body positivity in the daylight
and cry over your curves at night?
Do you go on and on about self-love
But secretly hate yourself?
~If 'yes'
The level of stupidity is achieved

You're prone to have a streak of hair on your body
Sometimes they scatter on your skin like raindrops
And sometimes try to sprout like flower bushes
On your head,
Between your legs,
Aloft your lips
Beneath your arms
~it's mandatory

Set a woman free
Yes, she's an untamed spirit
But she carries the essence of a mother within
Even if she roams around every society and civilization
She will come home to share what she's learned

Oh, dear heart! How can I speak of feminism?
When I see her victory as my failure
How can I lecture others to change?
When I failed to do on my own
For that I'll try to understand
The women around me
Are my sisters
Not my rivals
~shame and step

She feels intensely
She thinks deeply
She loves fiercely
She sequesters brutally
Her tears flow unconditionally
As her laughter
Her absence is as powerful
As her presence
She's an oyster with the heart of a pearl
Like her, there is no other in the world
You can't find her unless she wants to be found
But when you do, you might not know her significance
Yet try not to lose her to your ignorance

saudade

(n.) a nostalgic longing to be near again to something or someone that's distant or that has been loved and then lost; 'the love that remains'.

A journey through the walked lanes
Footprints and traces on the leaves
Sense streams with delight and pleasure
Heart yearns for fond relics and remembrance
Time is moving, so am I
Yet soul was stuck all the while
A faceless silhouette was chasing me
It's the nostalgia whispering 'set me free'

One summer evening we're walking hand-in-hand as the sun sets

Through the crowded road of the Jawahar Streets

We paused at the toy mart

Where I cried for the one in my height

Your glance refused; my lips pouted

You said 'no, not that,' I launched my regular rocket

Tears stung my eyes, and your heart melted like ice

I got my ruby plushie with a hat draining your glittering pochette

You were about to get my new friend boxed

But I wanted to take her on a piggyback ride

Everyone on our way watched me agape

As I held up a toy of my height around my skinny nape

You might be mad at the nights I would spend holding her close

Yet I'd swear you and her are the ones I never want to lose

Pretty toy, loving mom, what shall the little me do?

But I know I had a perfect day with you

White shirt, black bottoms
Dark shades and dim cap
Your hand untangling my hair
I was convinced the world was fair

New language, fresh concept
The blockbuster movie, mid seat
Sleep in my orbs, me in your arms
You left the things unsaid, promises wordlessly kept

First-ever bike raid, snacks store in a stride
Bills were pushed, marshmallows were pulled
The taste still on my tongue, the scar still in my mind
How could you ignore it when you're the one who taught me to be kind?

One clown, a bunch of colours, a lot of work
Closing deadline for a summer school homework

Everything in the world is sealed with a price tag
Every time it's not the money
Sometimes they are broken hearts and
traumatized minds

You're that
black and white moment
that flashes in front of my eyes
when I listen to my
favourite song,
That one scene
from my favourite movie
that lives in my mind
rent-free,
One song I heard
in the morning
I murmur throughout
the entire day
~a delightful deception

Whenever I look into a mirror, I look at her
She, who lost who she is
Trying to become who she should be

To the girl, I know
Who is too sensitive
Or too considerate
Tell her I miss her

To the girl, I know
Who is a little too private
Or over shares everything
Tell her I miss her

To the girl, I know
Who stays up late for birthdays
Who is the one standing in her own way
Tell her I miss her

To the girl, I know
Who either sends a long paragraph
Or forget to reply for year's
Tell her I miss her

To the girl, I know

To the girl, I know
Who is a little too much of everything
Or is little too less than being enough
Tell her I miss her

Not because she learned the concept of stability
She's still in the intuition of extremes
No one taught her of 'in-between'
But she lost herself anyhow being on the edge
Trying to balance on the breaking bridge
To the girl, I was once before
Tell her I miss her

To the girl who's
Dancing to her favourite song
Living in a world where zero goes wrong
Getting everything without searching for
Yet throwing tantrums for the attention of all
To the girl, I once were
Tell her I miss her

As a child, I often daydream about the time when I'll be an adult. I had it all planned, every event was scheduled, and every move of mine was schemed. There was a timeline for all my adventures, for all the men and miracles I'll be a part of. I assumed what I would be in certain years and how I react to that. I had my whole life dotted like a map. Continents to travel, mountains to trek, oceans to voyage, finally, synagogue to pilgrimage. Who will be my companions, and how long they'll be? Who will stay? Who will leave? Who will live? Who will die?

And then the sun came up and reality set in. The younger died, the older lived. Some friendships I wished for in life turned out to be toxic. The last ones I expected to start a conversation with came out to be the best thing that happened. The white coat and Steth I yearned to possess were replaced with the ink and quill, prescription turned out to be my manuscripts.

The castle of my assumptions was, discoloured, bruised, and scraped stone by stone, my skin was shredded layer by layer. The more parts I lose, the closer I came to my true self.

Universe staged a script in the theatre of my life, my mind was blown and the thoughts were

Lost:
I lost the person I used to be
Search:
I search for the person I am supposed to be
Forgot:
I forgot the person I want to be

You fall in love with the people
Who makes you feel certain things or doesn't
~there is no in-between

My time with you was like a pattern of clouds
I know it will vanish one day
But that doesn't make it any less beautiful

Time is fragile
Time is arcane
Every time I lost you
I flip the hourglass around
I didn't let the sand settle down
This time, I want you to do the same

No elegy can eulogize
The way you built my hope
Or the way you shattered it

I want to hold on
You want to let go
Sometimes things fall back together
And fall apart on the other
Time passed; years crossed
Here again, we are still walking the same lane
Somewhere none of us wants to compromise

Skeleton in the closet shivering for a skin
Feet that shod light should dance
Right people wrong timing
Never had the luxury of second chance

She's a secret keeper kept in secret

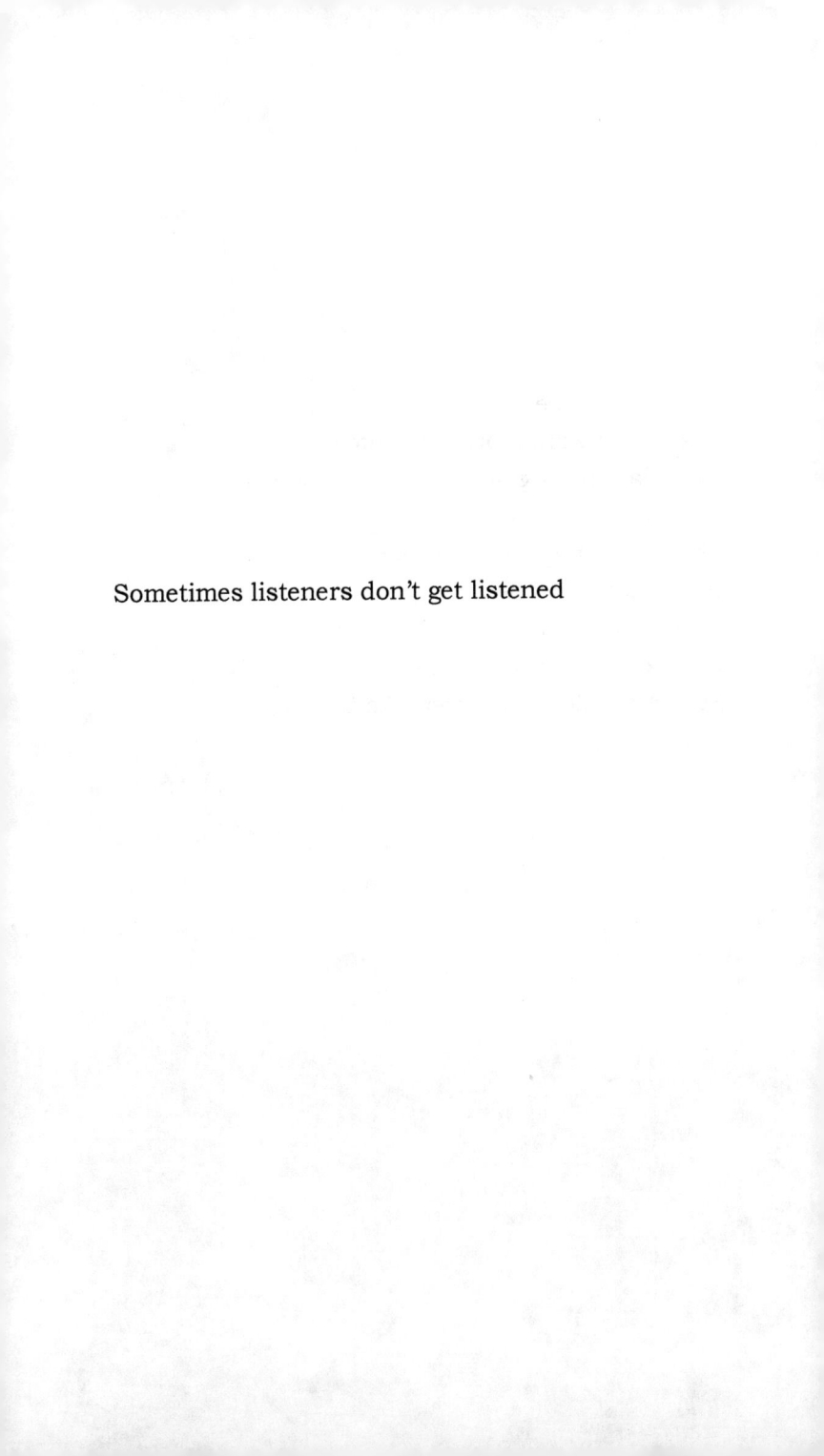

Sometimes listeners don't get listened

She's a bad poetry
Misspelled words, broken sentence
Irregular spacing, jagged punctuation
But when you read her out
She has a story that makes sense
It's hard to read her
Either you fail at the first sentence
Else you'll never reach the end
~some people are doomed like that

We strolled through the lanes of my soul
I showed you unicorns and rainbows
Crystal castles, secret tunnels
Radiant red roses and lancing thorns
Coffee houses and sad prose
Auroras and poetries
Birds cooed your name
Wild beasts so tame
But be fooled not my, Liebe,
I had shown you a vision
Of what you lose
If you
Betrayed
Me
Yet, somehow you did

Salt and turmeric
Both maims your wound
One to hurt you
The other to heal you
~be careful who you let in

Loving someone toxic
Is like breathing through water
Not everyone can do it
It takes a lot of constant efforts,
You have to survive a lot of struggles
You might be a skilled swimmer
But have to get out of it
If not,
At one point,
You'll be choked

After an extent
It's not the fear of losing you
That holds me back
It's the fear of losing the parts of me
That's embedded to yours

Silence
What's supposed to be sedated.
Calm all the hurricanes inside,
Bring solace to my soul
Is quite the thing
That haunts me the most
Is it the chasm of the memories we created?
Else the souvenir of this estranged alienation?
'Cause in the lull of darkness
The absence of your footstep
Is the only sound that wakes me up

Days, when her face was a band of crystals bright, were now gone

By the rivers and woods in the dew-locks of night, later the shades were drawn

She stood in shadow weeping beneath her car's light

She isn't a fallen arrow, indeed a scarred starlight

Then I fought for my feelings
Now I fight with them
I had not a sole idea
I grow up so fast
Just to break

I miss the days
When I know every trivial detail of her life
And she knows every detail of mine
We were separated by college, places, and time
Particularly in the event of adulation
The adulthood had marinated us,
The endless conversation in the restroom
Zestful banter about who said it first
White lies in the preparation for exams
Careless walk in the corridor, arriving late to the class
Murmuring in the morning assembly
Watching each other's posture while singing the national anthem
Shouting each other's names when their crush crosses
Changing bench and coming back were our
'Built to fall apart and fall back together'
Communicating the expectation of a life partner
Choosing names for each other's kids
Depressing about being the youngsters
Pre-booking to be the bridesmaid and godmother

Immiscible—the parts of me
I want to be seen; I want to be heard
Yet I always try to hide
I have strong opinions, I have indifferences
I crave the spotlight, I lurk in the twilight
I'm stuck-up, I'm insecure
I'm stubborn, I'm indecisive
I'm a perfectionist
I'm a procrastinator
Blake's innocence and experience
Is the essence of my existence
I'm black, I'm white
I'm a grey-shaded satellite

Our minds erase the traumas
to help us move on
If only our bodies are so much
considerate
there will be no scars

If only my body is
that forgetful
I won't be alarmed
anytime my body thinks
danger is coming
I would be in peace

If only my body is
oblivious, not be
A constant reminder

Lest I felt the agony of the losing someone dear
Whispering verses of love and hope yearning you'd hear
Watching the shooting star, wishing you were here
Imprinting footnotes from porch to terrace I'd swear
Building temple in your arms, your name, a sacred prayer
Foolish maiden's wishful thinking; wishing you would reappear
Hopes were hunted, peace was poached,
Nights were haunted, days were ambushed
Yet you stayed disappeared
Yet you stayed disappeared

Painted smiles, stained tears
Broken tiles, labelled chairs
Dancing with my hands tied
Walking with my legs tugged
The script, the backdrop
I walk, I talk, I hop
The voice, the words, the song
I'm chained to a cord all along
The days I felt my flesh and bone
Are nothing less than long gone
The ever-changing dusk and dawn
Life goes on until the curtains are drawn
I'm in a world, I've never known
I move but not on my own
In the royal nest, I craved for a wing
Unknown; I'm the puppet on a string

A word, a phrase, a memory—
A trivial thought becomes a sublime
Roots into my nerves gnawed my bones
Spreads its branches all around my sanity and sense
As vintage vine around my mind
Somehow, they are all intertwined
A monstrous tree, snake-like branches—
As it takes the shape, comes to life
Her ebony wings embraced the breathing wind out
Wood-to-wood, a forest fire is all I could think about
Viola turned to wisteria; I didn't move for so long
Red drops on her wings; it bleeds underneath my scars all along
The trivial thought, broke me down, freezing my ground
Sunniest star in my town, my beloved
Take me home, beneath the land buried in leaves
Else under her wing, in this familiar darkness let

hiraeth

(n.) a homesickness for home which you cannot return, a home which maybe never was; the nostalgia, the yearning, the grief for the lost places of your past.

I'm a traveller without a map
~lost

Nothing matters what people say, or do
Nothing matters what changed or who
Nothing matters what you watch or read
Nothing matters what you thread or shed
Nothing matters day or night, dark or bright
At one point in your life, you'll regret not being right
You'll regret the birthdays and holidays you missed
The conference and convocation you skipped
You'll regret not watching me grow up
In the time you didn't bother to show up
You stormed out of my life
When I was the house of cards
Here I'm shattered like a shards
Without a hint or regards
If you decide to abandon your child
Running her fragile soul all riled
Then isn't it apparent,
That you don't have anything left to call yourself

What's an illusion?
It's when you stare at an ocean
All you see is blue
But it's actually colourless

A soul with a void
A heart where emotions devoid
Is like a highness' empty banquet
Else when a bank of emotion is bankrupt

"Love is like an ocean. It's endless,"
someone said once
"Love is like an ocean. There is an end. We fail to see it."
~a broken heart whispered

Loving means allowing someone in

Allowing a person in means letting your guards down

Letting your guards down means you have to stay open,

Feel everything intensely, be vulnerable

And vulnerable hearts open to the deepest wounds

In the home of life
I'm in the darkest room
Imprisoned,
Strangled,
Deserted

In the home life
I'm in the darkest room
Latched shut
By people's expectations
Of what I feel, how I react
Who I should be,
The windows were sealed
Concealing the glints of light
From reaching out to me—who's
Haunting the same corner
For months now

Maybe I walked out of the womb with it
An exhausted body, withered soul
A melancholic spirit

From which I'm running from, with dear life
'Cause in the home of life
I'm in the darkest room
~when the void emerged?

Showing your vulnerability
Is a great bonding aspect
Unless the other one
Starts to play with it,
Or takes you for granted,
Your emotion might be your strength
Your emotion might be your weakness
Never tolerate anyone to play with it
Letting your guards down is okay
Only until the person on the other side
Points the sword at you.
~lesson learned

Some tunnels don't have light at the end of it,
Sometimes they are just a dark hollow space
And just like that,
Some people are just who they are

The thing about pain is
It consumes;
When you feel
It consumes you
When you don't
It consumes your way

The abuse is a physical aspect
~the biggest misconception

Too scared to let go
Too broken to hold on
~some people are doomed that way

I want it all to end
But it pulls me back in
~the vicious circle of life

"Why are you running? What are you running from?"

I run fast

With all my strength

With all the courage

Towards a dwindling destination

I don't know what I am running from

But I still keep running

I don't know where I'll end up

But I still keep running

For that, I may not end up in a better place

But I know I don't wanna stay

'Because if I stay, I will try to hold on

If I try to hold on then I'll realize there is nothing left

Here I go again

Just from where I began

Ever felt invisible and yearn to disappear at the same time?

~the story my life

Isolation is the most terrific poverty
~the scarcity of love

The baggage of our lives
Seeks shelter in the bags beneath our eyes

If chaos is the magma, then my mind is a volcano

Pity those who overthink everything

For that, they are cursed, with their own imagination

I want to love you
I want to try again
I'll wait for you to change
I'll try to stay a little longer
I'll try to try a little harder
I ain't sure how to leave
I have nowhere else to go
~me to my body

"Aren't you ready to accept me as I am?" My body asked me

"I'm asking the world for the same" I replied

I let my mind
To get on my nerves
~where it all started

Anything in excess is a poison
Even your own thoughts are no exception

Dehydrated body
Exhausted thoughts
Shrivelled heart
Wilted soul
Yearning to be tucked in bed
Yet here I am screaming stuck in head
~story of a silent scream in summer and stress

Butterflies in your stomach
Shiver down your limbs
Sweat on your palms
Desert in your throat
Voices in your head
Fear in your mind
~anxiety

Silence
You crave when in group
You hate when left alone in

Familiar as the childhood acquaintance
Personal as the secret chest behind the bedpost
Makes the heart flutter, the words stutter like a lover
Turns up every time without a proposal
Sweat in palms, butterflies in stomach,
Shiver in limbs, invisible beast
Sharp teeth, strong jaw
Tossing the diaphragm like a taj ball
Breathe races, chest heaves
Stays even when everyone leaves
~anxiety

Silence at first
A deafening scream at the end
~depression

Quietly loud
Silent scream
Invisible sword
Slivering the limbs
Dangling off the side of a building
My hand is going to slip any second
~anxiety feels like

One kingdom, three heirs
Combatting for the throne
Battling for the spot of their own
All in one, trying to overthrow the other
Parts of the same building blocks
Disconnected as different walls
~body, heart and mind

I'm a bird in a golden cage
Confined by the towers of
Expectations, boundaries, perspective
Eagle-eyed spectators assessing my wings
Debating how much I have to put on and give
Trapped words, with a sheer will to run
Certain chances are a million to one
Chaotic heart striving to fly screaming, 'screw it'
Yet here I am left with no emergency exit

metanoia

(n.) the journey of changing one's mind, heart, self, or the way of life.

I tried to scream; my mouth was taped shut
Cries muffled, shrieks stifled, no sound left
After months and years, cracks and tears
Here I go again trying to scream with my fingertips
~can you hear me?

The thing about solitude is
I can't tell it's healing or hurting me
or both?
~question of my life

It's important to have your illusions shattered to recognize the reality

Dwelling on my past
Romanticizing the bygones
Fretting about my future
Distressing on the destiny
Bypassing the only moment that's real
It's no wonder I don't feel alive
~discovering the roots

I'm a first draft
Crafted raw and pure
From the unleashed imagination
Holding the unwielded emotions
No polished phrases
Else literary devices
Plenty of flaws
Words to strikeout,
Phrases to alter
POV to re-check
Darlings to cut off
Changes to be made
Whacked with criticism,
Roaming in reluctance
A few qualms to abandon,

I sat beneath the velvet sky
aloft the meadow pasture
fondling my knees
cuddling my limbs
With the warble of gusting wind,
the sound of birds communicating
in their covert tongue
I rest my chin on my knee pad
cherishing the Midas touch of Zephyr
My gaze becomes the southern pole to the northern star
Lungs filled with oxygen
Mind crammed with solace
The knots in my soul eased
like a baby's first yawn
Somewhere in between
the solitude embraced me

Never break a poet's heart
She will inscribe and engrave the pain and heal
You will skim and scan through them and bleed
Never break a poet's heart
She'll swear with synecdoche, mocks with metaphor
She'll pen her grief on her manuscript,
Remembering all the moments when sadness crept
She dusts the rhymes and schemes like the stars on the blue
That tug at your heart 'cause it's you
Your actions never matched your words
Your promises never harmonized with your efforts
Never break a poet's heart
Yes, her words are magical
Yet they will cut through your skin like the sword
You can't comprehend that it's sweet disposition
Else slow venomous potion

There's another tunnel at the end of one
Sometimes the bravest thing to do is run
Relationships are not a stunt
Change is the only constant
Some losses set you free
Black and white will never cease to be
Merry or misery will fleet away one day
One day or the other you'll learn to walk away
Parents are just normal people
Toxic people will always be lethal
Permanent is a lie
Everything that lives will die
Some people will remain gone
Against all the odds life goes on
~Some truths of life

Some of the cages were mental
Wounds are not just physical
To abuse is not love
Toxicity can't be cured
Broken things can't be fixed
Some people are just who they are

What does depression feel like?

It feels like you are in a shipwreck, with no land in sight. Water seeps in through every crack you didn't attend to. It makes you sort of gasp for air. You'll search for a railing to hold on to but the flow of current pulls you in. Once you are inside the water. Drowned. It takes you for a spin. Tossing and throwing you from head to toe and vice versa. The mercurial melody of the water striking every cell in your body intoxicating you that your almost lost the track of time or the thought of a refugee. Once in a while, you'll reach the surface as the universe will remind you to keep expecting a land. You'll be forced to focus on land and it's the hardest thing to do. By that time your body will be frozen and all you see is blue. You've been consumed. If you give in to the easiest, you'll end up sinking into the bottom of the ocean. But if you try a little

I'll stop saying
'Mental illness'
When they stop screaming
'It's all in your head'

People always say,
'Let go'
'Move on'
But don't,
Stay
Hold on
Let the emotions consume you
Drown you
Drain you
Get sick of you
And eventually, get rid of you
Just remember its possible
Only if you have
a little hope in-between

During the lockdown
Everyone shut their doors
She opened her heart
They were in loneliness
She was in solitude
They were in chaos
She was in tranquillity
They felt imprisoned
She ran wild exploring herself
They had all the time but nothing to do
She had time to do everything she wanted to
Walls, calls, and texts; their life
Poetry, music, and movies; her world
They were drilled, she was thrilled
It trapped them in greyscale but painted her golden
'Cause in lockdown

For once in my life
I wish to be a poem, not a poet
I don't want to coin catchy phrases,
Built a lyrical narration,
Sync the causes with simile
Clothe the sentence with metaphors
I want to be draped in the velvet and silk of magnificent words
For once, I don't want to write
For once, I want to be written about
For once, I want to be a receiver
For once, I want to be a muse
For once, I want to be loved
For once, I want to be a poetry
For once in my life

(Read it backwards)

Brooding over your past mistakes is like re-reading the same book and expecting a different climax

Some people write for fun
And some to intend a pun
Words aren't a misfired bullet from a gun
Their flow is indeed a million to one

Some people write to express
Some in the desire to impress
Their words would be freshly fitted nevertheless
Crossing the boundaries of the people's eerie guesses
Yes, there will be combating agents of stress
Yet people be happy to have what they possess

Yet these thoughts don't repulse so light
Some people though write;

Not for pleasure,
Or for leisure,

'Cause if the words aren't written
They sting like a wound—leather-bitten
Some words are painful and forbidden

Gush through your minds like wilful wild birds
It sprouts with the delicacy of the first bud
Crashing their sleep with a Zeus's thud
You might suffer some snarling
But don't mistake them, Darling
'Cause some words are safer
When they are on the paper

I wished for
My disturbing traumas
Painful memories to be erased
But here I am relishing them with sheer passion
~'walking contradiction' is my middle name

Wrath of the blaze to chisel the metal
The severity of the snow to crave some warmth
The acerbity of the sun to shine your days
Likewise, the emotion of an poet to inscribe a poetry
~dynamic

Some secrets gossip through the fingertips

She held the universe in her soul
Cascaded stars on her manuscripts
~every writer ever

Who said pain is not beautiful?
I vent it out with verses

I write to taste my life twice
Smile for the same happiness twice
Mourn the same grief twice
Laugh about the same joke twice
Feeling the gain and loss twice
Cherish the same memories twice
Live my whole life once again
With a tinge of hyperbole
And a hue of imagination
In the moment and retrospect

"What am I to you?"
"You're every dream of my nights pushes me asleep
And every hope of my mornings pulls me awake."
~me and my words

Dear inspiration,
Come back to me
I've been missing your melody
Striking around my mind and body
Stimulating my sense
Exhilarating my essence

Come back to me
My thoughts are deserted
My ink is dried up
The flame of passion dwindling
Yearning for just a tiny kindling

Come back to me
Drape me,
In the smooth silk of wild words
Twirl me,
In the breeze of gentle havoc
Bathe me,
In the velvet flow of creativity
Ignite me,

If words are passion
Silence is peace
One flies like wilful birds
Other bounds with ease

Open wounds heal in silence
The scars gossip through words
Real feelings felt in silence
Expressed through words

Dark fears conquered in silence
Motivation seeps through words
Unending battles fought in silence
The victories are eulogized in words

Confusions conclude in silence
Clarity shared through words
Words provoke you to expect
Silence allows you to accept

Words are inciting

Whenever they asked me
to cut the tie with toxicity,
I have always seen my surroundings
not within me
And that's a mistake
To get rid of the toxicity outside
I had to cleanse the ones within me

The first step to cleansing your body and mind is
To let go of the things that have served
Their purpose in your life
~men or materials

Cleanse yourself
No one's gonna do it for you
Even the snow washes itself
By itself

What's self-love if we can't embrace the darkest parts of ourselves?

No one's opinion influences you
more than that of your own
the change begins within you
~where the change began

I accepted that happiness
Has nothing to with
Being happy
All the time
~where it changed

sophrosyne

(n.) a healthy state of mind, characterized by self-control, moderation, and a deep awareness of one's true self, and resulting in true happiness.

Ever wondered why everything bad happens to you?
Because it's your story,
You are the main character
And you have the ability and choice to change it
~change your story

Some things in life
Are not meant to be
Fully understood
Just like some people
~to all the men and miracles

'Broken'
Another way of saying
The elements of what's being created

You can't have a home
If you feel unsettled with yourself

Emotion is a volcano
The longer you suppress it
The deeper it depresses you
Hiding your emotion doesn't make you strong
Showing your emotion doesn't make you weak
Sometimes you have to break down to breakthrough

Don't pity the one who's in pain
Pity the one who didn't
For that they are cursed to feel the death in the living
~the fortune of feeling pain

I found myself
In the dancing wind chains
Multi-coloured, over my cradle
In the sound of my name and claps
Applauds, cheers, and yells
Like I achieved tons of gold medals

I found myself
In the joy of my parents,
Bittersweet dinners with my family,
The toys and teddy I played
The crowd of kins and folks lined,
To know the reason why I whined

I found myself
In nature, the thing around me
In the first drop of the rain
The prolonged whistle of the train
The smell of the freshly bloomed rose
And the sight of the sun and moon when they rose

Until it faded into a hilarious tragedy
In the memories we created
In the realities we distorted

I found myself
In the broken promises, people that fled
The moments that are no more left
The laughs and light that faded
In the tears and darkness that shrouded
Leaving me with nothing but memories
Haunting and hunting my nights and days

I found myself
In my mind, sense, and sanity
That's become the demon that haunts me to the eternity
In endlessly overthinking everything
Until there is nothing left to surprise or shock
Except for the tears puddled behind my lock

I found myself
In the screaming silence of solitude

The conflict and clash consumed me like a quicksand
I dread every moment of it,
Every moment I spent consumed in that pit

I found myself
Trying to find my way over it
Until I realized I should go through it,
Burying myself deep down
So that I can sprout and bloom
Amid all the unearthing and thriving
A realization flowered;
Solitude can too be soothing

I found myself
In the feet of light and love
In the baby steps towards self-love
Rummaging through past and present
For a spark to fuel my soul
A match to blew my mind
A flame to manifest my fascination
An ember to illume my passion

In the delicacy of the language
In the silk threads of emotions
Weaved with the sequins of perspective
Literary devices scattered on the lines like the stars in the sky
In poetries, the ink-stained pages
And the matters of the heart it held through the ages

I found myself
Reading between the lines
Tears and smiles in the make-believe lives
Hiding behind the words of the book
In coffee fragrant libraries
In all the fictional realities

I found myself
In my unleashed imagination
In my thriving creativity
The portal to another reality
Penning down my myths and tales
With a unique disposition, sharp pen, and a thin skin

There is no darkness without a ray of light
There is no brightness without a dash of night
Amid all the dusk and dawn
Live 'cause the life goes on

Even if it crashes and burn
The ashes of efforts will be colourful

Your heart hasn't been broken by a single incident or a person

But a series of tiny pain you neglected

There is a contribution of every person in deepening the initial crack

It will heal the same way too

~it's healing now

Some experiments will turn to experience

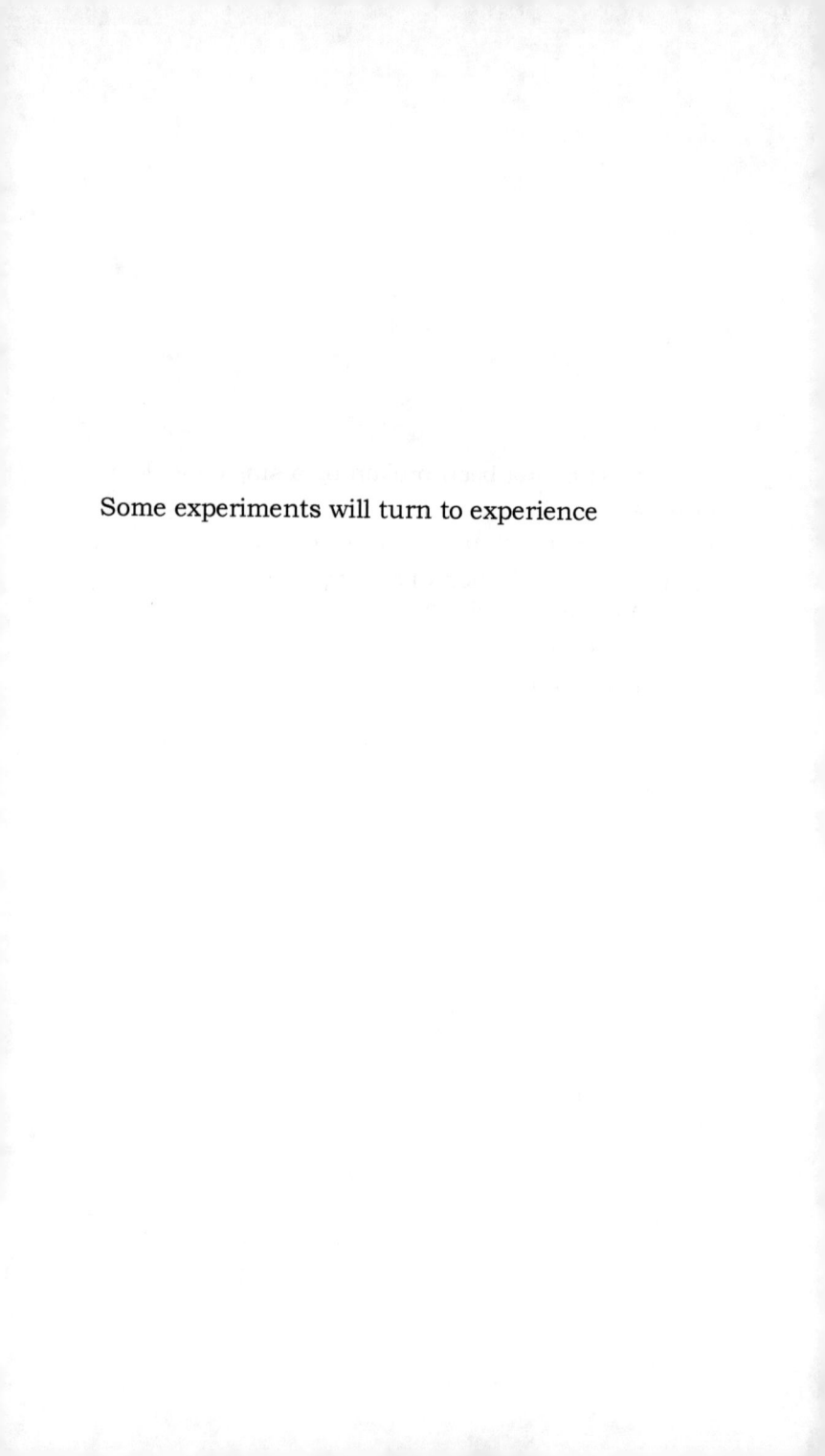

The weight of hate,
Self-loath,
The burden of hating
The home
My soul lives in
It's exhausting

My soul is too sensitive to toxicity

You are a diamond
Even after severing the useless parts,
bruiting to the specific shape,
cleansing,
and polishing,
you have flaws
you have imperfections
And that's what makes you authentic
That's what makes you beautiful

You and a character from a book have
Personality and perspective
Strengths and weaknesses
Perfections and flaws
Friends and family
Merry and misery
Past and future
In the end, all that matters
To grasp the happy ending,
Is your belief in them
~an epiphany

My soul is my home
Take off your shoes, wipe your feet at the door
Let everything else slip off, watch your step
Don't touch anything fragile,
Just keep an eye on those minute details
I'll let you in and let you out with grace
But promise me, darling, to leave no prints or trace

Sooner or later
The timing will be right,
The stars will be aligned,
We will find a love that stays
That heals us
Sometimes in a person
Sometimes in a purpose
Sometimes in ourselves

You drenched me like a pre-monsoon rain
~self-love

Black has taught me
That even by being nothing
You can be something

My life is chronic chaos of 'why' and 'what if'

~if we cease to question the odds, why would we want to live?

The first draft is vulnerable
An incomplete masterpiece
Skin to shed
Core to discover
The fragility makes it beautiful
The flaws make it fascinating
The first piece of an art
Indeed, carries a special piece of heart

You are made of stardust
It's no wonder you feel like
Exploding when you're in
Pleasure or pain
It takes a nebula,
A cosmic storm,
A celestial cyclone,
Plenty of catastrophe
In a synonymous volume
For a star to be born
Whenever you feel like
Breaking or exploding
Remember it's time
For the star
To be born
Creating a star
A revolution
Is not because someone else wants you to
It's something you are born to do

Feeling intense emotions isn't a crime but humane
Criticism isn't a rock but the jewel on my crown
All the cages were my mind's trick
Now my words are wild and possess wings
~the realization

You won't plant the seeds today
And foresee for the flowers to bloom tomorrow
Yet why you feel unworthy
If you are not working long enough
Or fast enough?
Magic doesn't happen that way
It takes time, consistent effort
Patience and forbearance
Amidst all the transition, just remember
There is nothing attractive than growing at your own pace

A dark corner I haunt
stemmed to be
The bright castle I dwell
The moment I realized
I don't belong to the
Past or future
But the present
~here and now is all I have

The elegance of living in the present
Is that you get to live with
This version of yourself
The one that's outgrown her past self
And growing into an even more competent self
~slow down and relish here while she's there

Begin you day with a smile
Watch the early morning sun
Listen to the birds chirping
Sipping your hot-brewed caffeine
Speak a little louder
Think a little deeper
Love a little harder
Live a little happier
Tap your feet for the rhythm of the rain
Humming your favourite tunes
Gaze at the late-night moon and stars
End your day with contentment
~you're where you're supposed to be

There is nothing in this world
Another person can give you
That you can't give your-self
There is no thirst in your body
That another person can quench
You can't quench yourself
There is no void in your soul
That another person can fill
That can't fill yourself
~you're your own person

One day I stopped searching
Neither thought nor action
I just want to be stagnant
Not move a limb
Laze around my bed all-day
There was nothing;
calls or mails,
tints or shades,
friends or family
comfort or community
Barely
The sound of my inner voice,
the warmth of my body
the tenderness of my thoughts
the fondness for my feelings
I fell deep into their dimensions

You can't please everyone, honey
Don't try
Human hearts are prone to discover
Faults in every star,
Flaws in every war,
Tangibility in chaos,
Treachery in a truce,
However
As long as you know your truth
As long as your actions synchronize with your conscience
As long as you cherish the person you wake up as
As long as you love the person in the mirror
As long as you remember what a miracle you are
Trust me, honey
You can find your serenity in any explosion

For once in your life
Uncondition your thoughts
Set your heart free
Unleash your soul

For once in your life
Let your thoughts
Snatch you out of your portrait
And paint your canvas,
With your wildest fantasies
Else fierce feelings and desires
In hues of exhilaration and euphoria

For once in your life
Let your heart
Take the lead
Swivel fearlessly,
Sweep you off your feet
And do what it does flawlessly

IN
THE
DARK

thoughts of a kind
in a modern mind
an ancient soul,
and a kid at heart
in a contemporary verse
she's a classical art
~this is she

She has always been my reflection
in joy,
leisure,
grief,
wrath,
vulnerability,
tears.
She's the one who made me who I am
completed my soul
She's the one who taught me to love
Without her, I've got no hand to hold
~my mom has always been my first best friend

loving you hasn't been easy
with all the things making me crazy
your Victories pleased me
your failures worried me
your laugh is the melody
your tears are the misery

you're the one i listen to
every time i'm blue
you're the one i seek
whenever i go weak
you saved me from my fear
there is no other I'd hear

a compliment on you made my day
an insult to you made me cry
my screams never reached your ears
yet, my dreams never left my eyes

the world stopped for a while
my heart goes an extra mile

i could never go tired
of the way you inspired
me. of the way i Admired
you. for that, i give my word
maybe the stars conspired
or the leaves transpired
my heart's been rewired
else the bullet misfired
i think i may be sired
darling, you are the one i desired

the moment you leave your car
i watched you from a million miles afar
from the screen of my window bar
being the one away from your memory jar
because of you, i learned to love my scar
darling, You're my northern star
~to my first and forever love

she is soft
she is free-spirited
she loves to call herself smart
even though she's not
she paints the world around her with hues of pink
she enjoys Japanese anime along with her video games
she never respected me
but she always loved me
she is adorable and precious
but she's also my stupid sister

I am a beach; people adore me from afar
species drown and float and hover
there were oysters
who bear precious pearls
rare to discover
but when I did, they were worth it

there were fishes
who stayed until someone stole them from me
there were seaweeds
who consumed every aspect of me
there were seashells
who after being my long-stayed guest
reached up to the shore

But then there were people

years ago, i fell in love with a girl
who made me Twist and turn and twirl
dressed in a white veil, she burned red
indeed, she's A rose in the thorn's bed

I knew I belong with her at that moment
the Young star-crossed Lovers reaped their fairy tale ending
she raised above all the mean comment
leading herself to greet the calm descending

she can be red, blue, black, and white Or golden
nevertheless, she chose to be a Rainbow
she can even a blank space gorgeous
making all those haters furious

she adores all the breeds of cats
though there is not enough time for purrs and pats
the day i listened to 'love story'
it embarked the beginning of our story

now that she Successfully carved her way

Flirting the strings of your guitar
you soothed all my silver scar
even being miles away you are one of the brightest stars
illuminating all my deepest, darkest hours
~the girl who loves Thirteen

Never seen your face, or caressed your skin
Still, your essence is familiar as the home I live in
You're the person I met for your likes and dislikes
Endorsed my fandoms, viewpoints, and interests
In the world of hugs and hand-holding
I felt your warmth through the screen and keyboard
~online friends are never really apart

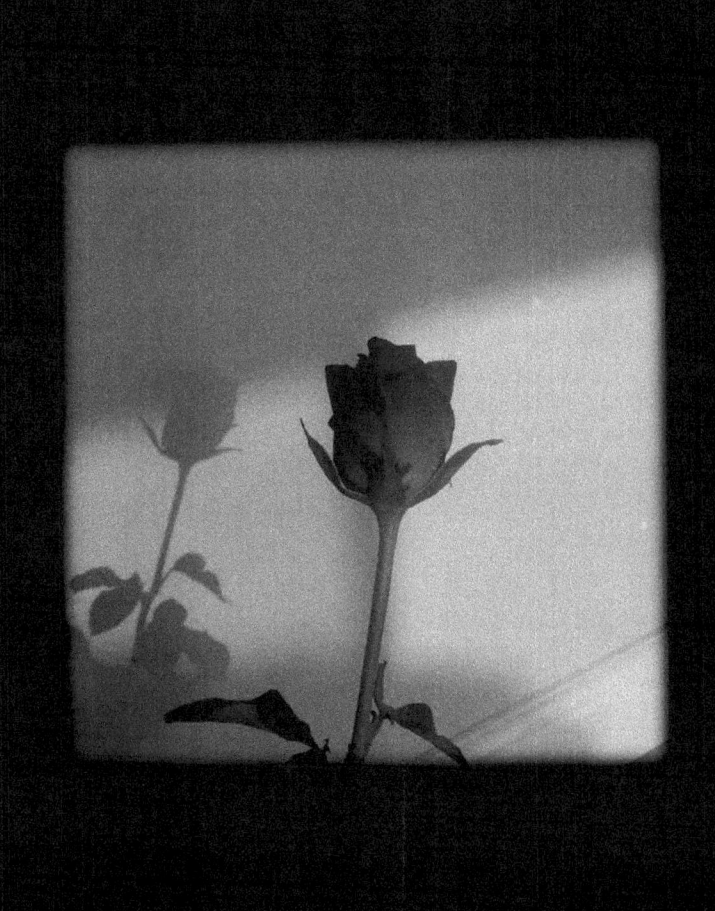

Akshaya is a juvenile writer with a shrewd personality and quick wit. She has a wanderlust to explore herself and the worlds of people around her. Rose-colored glasses contemplating her monochrome mind she prevails unique. Fancies stars, desires fiction, lives in fantasy with no time for any fallacy. Solely obsessed with morally grey characters with a redemption arc. Loves to analyze every little thing in life either for good or not so. Writes from her personal experience with a tinge of hyperbole and imagination. She takes fifteen years of her life to fall in love with the words and never expects to fall out of it. The art of writing is something that could keep her on her toes, and give her a sense of control. Throughout her life, writing became an extension of her being. Loves music, books, and movies. Hates judgy people, narrow mindsets, and blind beliefs.

~about the author

Rants about music, books, movies, Harry Potter, TVD, and any American TV shows? Please crash into my message box.

My worst nightmare;
Being naked in the crowd,
Every inch of me unveiled to the world
It doesn't scare me anymore
'Cause something happened
Something like never before
A vagary
A hygge
An impulse to be a virago
A saudade
A hiraeth
A metanoia
A sophrosyne
A journey towards acceptance
An excursion to healing
I embraced the darkest carton in my soul
The light was in there, buried in silence
Loitering to be unlocked
Once it was undone

Printed in the USA
CPSIA information can be obtained
at www.ICGtesting.com
LVHW020528041123
762971LV00060B/1017

9 789356 282940